8/01

E

NANCY FARMER

RUNNERY GRANARY

PICTURES BY
JOS. A. SMITH

GREENWILLOW BOOKS, NEW YORK

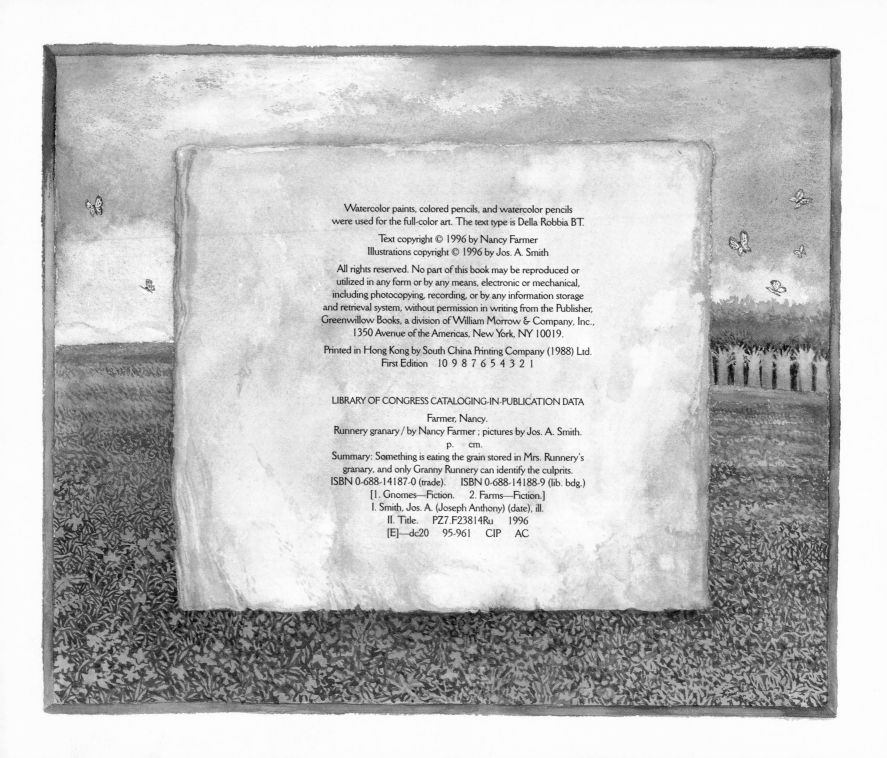

Watercolor paints, colored pencils, and watercolor pencils
were used for the full-color art. The text type is Della Robbia BT.

Printed in Hong Kong by South China Printing Company (1988) Ltd.
First Edition   10 9 8 7 6 5 4 3 2 1

LIBRARY OF CONGRESS CATALOGING-IN-PUBLICATION DATA

Farmer, Nancy.
Runnery granary / by Nancy Farmer ; pictures by Jos. A. Smith.
p.   cm.
Summary: Something is eating the grain stored in Mrs. Runnery's
granary, and only Granny Runnery can identify the culprits.
ISBN 0-688-14187-0 (trade).   ISBN 0-688-14188-9 (lib. bdg.)
[1. Gnomes—Fiction.   2. Farms—Fiction.]
I. Smith, Jos. A. (Joseph Anthony) (date), ill.
II. Title.   PZ7.F23814Ru   1996
[E]—dc20   95-961   CIP   AC

FOR
HAROLD

—N. F.

FOR
SUSAN AND AVA—
thank you,
thank you,
thank you

—J. A. S.

Mr. Runnery had a mill by a stream. As the water went by, it turned a great wheel. The wheel turned the mill, and the mill ground the grain into flour.

Mrs. Runnery had a granary on a high hill. It was built out of stone, and the roof was of iron. The granary was full of grain, from bottom to top. The windows were locked to keep out the things that ate grain.

When the cold winter came, the farmers knocked on Mrs. Runnery's door. They said, "Please give us the grain we have stored. We must take it down to the stream to be ground by the mill into flour."

Year after year it had been so.

But one day Mrs. Runnery looked in her granary and found some of the grain missing.

"I must have weevils," she said. "What can I do about weevils?"
She never used poison. It might get into the grain and hurt the farmers.
"Try spiders, try spiders," said Hillary Runnery, the older daughter.

So the Runnerys went to the woods
and caught cages of spiders—
cages and cages and cages of spiders!

When they opened the cages in the granary, the spiders ran up the walls, all over the walls!

"Ugh!" said Mrs. Runnery. Still, it was better than poison.

The next morning Mrs. Runnery opened the door and found the spiders clinging to the ceiling in a bunch. Their webs were slashed to smithereens, every one!

"There's something bigger than weevils in this granary," she said.

"We must have rats."

She fetched the cages, and the spiders ran back inside. They were eager to get away.
The Runnerys took the spiders to the woods and turned them loose.

"Try cats, try cats," said Valery Runnery, the younger daughter.
So the Runnerys went to the farmhouses and borrowed the cats.

The farm cats were big and tough. They yowled and lashed
their tails as they were let into the granary.
"Now we'll see some action," said Mrs. Runnery.

The next morning Mrs. Runnery found the cats clinging to the ceiling by the tips of their claws. They streaked out the door, going back to their farms.

"I must have something really big in this granary," she said.

"I can't imagine what it is."

Mrs. Runnery called the whole family together.

"Wolves," said Mr. Runnery.

"Wolves don't eat grain," Hillary said.

"Cows," said Mrs. Runnery.

"Cows don't scare cats," Valery said.

"I know what it is."
They all turned toward the fireplace, where Granny Runnery was rocking in a chair and toasting her toes.

"You've got gnomes," said Granny. "Gnomes go after grain like bears after honey. You'd better get rid of them before they clean the place out."

"I don't want to use poison," said Mr. Runnery.

"Poison! Poo!" said Granny. "The gnomes put poison on their bread like peanut butter. It won't even give them a stomach ache."

"I don't want to use traps," said Mrs. Runnery.
Granny laughed harshly. "The only thing you'd catch in a trap
is your fingers. Gnomes are much too clever for that."

"Then what can we do?" cried Hillary and Valery.
"The only way to get rid of them is to use gnome paper,"
Granny said. "Fortunately, I know just how to make it.

"Get hiccups and honey and hair.
Get money and marbles and meat.
Go out to the woods in the moonlight.
And glue the whole mess to a sheet."

The Runnerys went out to the woods that night.
They laid out a big, strong sheet of paper in the moonlight.
Mr. Runnery poured honey over it. Mrs. Runnery sprinkled
it with money, marbles, and meat, and Valery cut off the
tips of her braids.

"What about the hiccups?" Hillary said.

"BOO!" shouted Granny.

Hillary was so startled, she got the hiccups. They landed on the paper and stuck to the honey.

"Good! Now we can hang it up," Granny said.

The granary was dark when the Runnerys tiptoed inside.
They heard scurrying feet and spooky laughter.

"Hang the gnome paper from the ceiling," ordered Granny.

An amazing sight greeted them in the morning! Gnomes were glued all over the paper. They were red and green and purple and blue. They had claws and horns and tails. Every one of them was fat as a pig from eating grain.

"What shall we do with them?" asked Mrs. Runnery.

"Put them in a boat and send them downstream," Granny said.
"They'll starve!" cried Mr. Runnery.
"Don't you believe it! By the time the moon rises tonight, the gnome paper will have fallen apart. That's how it is with gnome paper. The hiccups eat holes in it."

Very carefully, the Runnerys picked up the gnome paper and put it into a boat. Away the boat went down the stream with the gnomes gnashing their teeth and complaining loudly.

When the moon rose, the gnome paper fell apart.
Grumbling, the gnomes made their way to shore
and set out to find another granary.

But the Runnerys never saw them again.